Date: 3/20/19

J 641.6374 KIM
Kim, Heather,
Beat it and bite it! : daring
and divine chocolaty

BEAT IT and BITE IT!

Daring and Divine Chocolaty Desserts

by HEATHER KIM

COMPASS POINT BOOKS
a capstone imprint

Chocolate Hazelnut
Peanut Butter Bars 10

Butterfinger® Flake Bars 12

Pretzel Peanut Butter Cups 14

Devil's Food Cake with
Chocolate Frosting and
Brownie-Streusel Crunch 18

Oreo® Crepe Cake 22

S'more Brownies 28

Chocolate Fudge with White
Chocolate Candied Ramen 36

Butterscotch Pudding Pots
with Chocolate Sauce 42

TABLE OF CONTENTS

Chocolate-Pretzel Tart with
Earl Grey Whipped Cream   32

Hot Chocolate Fondue   44

SAME INGREDIENT, SASSY NEW TWIST

Dark, milk, or white, in candies, sauces, and cakes—there are endless ways to enjoy chocolate. Do you like baking and cooking with this beloved ingredient but need some fresh ideas? Then you're in luck.

Surprising flavor combinations, such as Earl Grey whipped cream and candied ramen noodles, will wow your taste buds. Mix in your favorite candy bars, like peanut butter cups and Butterfinger® bars, to make new sweet treats with a traditional twist. From fondue to cakes with a crunch, these daring, divine recipes are sure to make every chocolate lover long for one more bite.

BAKING IT SAFE

Baking can be adventurous and fun, but even more so when you stay safe in the kitchen. Follow these tips to help make sure your desserts don't turn dangerous.

Always wash your hands before you begin baking, if you spill, and after touching eggs.

Use caution when handling sharp objects. Ask for an adult's help when a recipe calls for chopping, slicing, or cutting. Hold the knife's handle firmly when cutting, and keep fingers away from the blade.

Also use caution when working near hot surfaces. Make sure an adult is nearby when operating the stovetop and oven at high temperatures. When using saucepans, turn the handles toward the center of the stove to avoid bumping a handle and spilling. Always wear oven mitts or pot holders while taking hot baking sheets or cake pans out of the oven.

Spills and messes are bound to happen. Wipe them up with paper towels or a damp kitchen towel to keep your countertop and floor clean and dry.

MIX IT UP

Before you gather up supplies and go shopping for ingredients, read through each recipe. Some recipes require waiting several hours or overnight for food to prepare. Make sure you plan accordingly.

Also make sure you know how to perform each technique. Here are a few common kitchen tools you will need and some baking procedures you will perform.

mixing bowl

electric mixer

food processor

mixing spoon

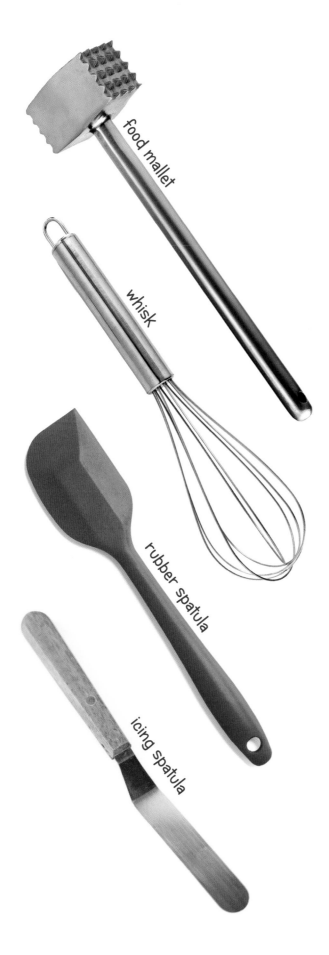

food mallet

whisk

rubber spatula

icing spatula

BEAT IT

Create a smooth, creamy mixture by stirring briskly, using a spoon, whisk, or mixer.

CREAM IT

Vigorously beat and stir ingredients. The result? Creamy, fluffy smoothness.

CRUMBLE IT

Crush food into tiny bits using a food processor or manual metal grinder.

DIVIDE IT

If an ingredient is "divided," you'll only use part of the total amount at one time.

GREASE IT

To grease a pan, use a stick of butter to thinly coat the inside of the pan. If you don't have butter, you can use cooking spray.

MELT IT

To melt chocolate, put it in a microwave-safe bowl and microwave for 1 minute. Remove and stir. Microwave for additional 15-second increments until smooth.

WHIP IT

Add air and volume to a mixture using a whisk or mixer.

WHISK IT

Use a whisk to combine ingredients using a side-to-side motion. If you don't have a whisk, use two forks.

CHOCOLATE AND PEANUT BUTTER, A DIVINE DUO

Whether it's smooth or chunky, salted or sweet, peanut butter is always delicious. But mixing peanut butter with chocolate? Now that's a match made in heaven!

CHOCOLATE HAZELNUT PEANUT BUTTER BARS

Part peanut butter, part hazelnut spread, totally fudgy, chocolaty, and delicious. You can't go wrong with these dessert bars that will hit everyone's sweet spot.

INGREDIENTS

1/2 cup butter, softened

1/2 cup peanut butter

1 cup brown sugar

1 egg

1 teaspoon vanilla extract

1 cup all-purpose flour

1/3 cup chocolate-hazelnut spread

1 Preheat oven to 350°F.

2 Grease an 8- by 8-inch (20- by 20-cm) baking pan with butter or nonstick cooking spray.

3 In a medium bowl, use a rubber spatula to mix the butter and peanut butter until fluffy.

4 Add the brown sugar. Mix until well-combined.

5 Add the egg and vanilla extract. Mix until well-blended.

6 Mix in flour until moist. Spread mixture into the prepared baking pan.

7 Drop the chocolate-hazelnut spread by spoonfuls into the pan. Using the back of a spoon, swirl it into the peanut-butter mixture. Rotate swirl patterns clockwise and counterclockwise.

8 Bake for about 30 minutes or until center is set and sides are golden.

9 Let cool completely. Cut into squares to serve.

BUTTERFINGER® FLAKE BARS

No one will flake on you if you're serving these Butterfinger® Flake Bars for dessert. These no-bake treats are part candy bar, part Rice Krispie Treat® with a decadent topping that's sure to be a crowd-pleaser.

BASE

1 16-ounce jar creamy peanut butter

1 cup dark chocolate chips

1/4 cup butter

1 cup Butterfinger®, crushed

3 cups rice flakes cereal, crushed

1/4 cup cocoa nibs

1 tablespoon salt

TOPPING

2/3 cup heavy cream

1 teaspoon vanilla extract

1 cup butterscotch chips

1 cup white chocolate chips

1 tablespoon kosher salt

1/2 cup granulated sugar

3 tablespoons butter

> **– SASSY TIP –**
> To scald, bring nearly to a boil and then cool down. "Caramelize" means to brown sugar with heat.

1. Grease a sheet pan with butter and line with a Silpat® mat or parchment paper. Set aside.

2. In a medium saucepan, melt the peanut butter, chocolate chips, and butter over low heat. Remove from heat. Stir in the Butterfinger®, cereal, cocoa nibs, and salt.

3. Spread mixture onto the prepped sheet pan, pressing firmly until solid and evenly spread.

4. Set aside until it reaches room temperature.

5. Meanwhile, make the topping. Scald cream and vanilla extract in a small saucepan. Set aside.

6. Place butterscotch chips, white chocolate chips, and salt in a medium bowl and set a strainer over the top.

7. In a separate saucepan, caramelize the sugar until it starts to smoke and becomes frothy. Remove from heat and immediately add butter, stirring until completely blended.

8. Pour this mixture over the strainer and onto the butterscotch and white chocolate chips.

9. Add scalded cream and vanilla to mixture and stir.

10. Immediately spread over the layer in the sheet pan until evenly distributed.

11. Top with additional crushed Butterfinger®, if desired. Serve at room temperature.

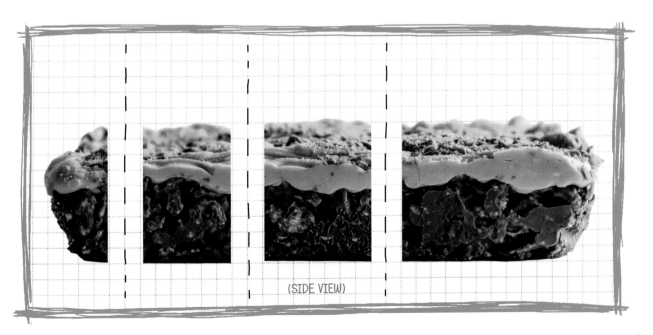

(SIDE VIEW)

PRETZEL PEANUT BUTTER CUPS

What's better than chocolate-covered pretzels? Chocolate-covered pretzels with peanut butter! These snacks are perfect for when you need a quick treat on the go.

INGREDIENTS

1/2 cup pretzels, crushed

1 1/4 cups semisweet chocolate chips

3/4 cup creamy peanut butter

1/4 cup powdered sugar

1/2 teaspoon vanilla extract

1/4 teaspoon kosher salt

1. Line a 24-cup mini muffin pan with mini cupcake wrappers. Evenly distribute the crushed pretzels among each cup.

2. Melt the semisweet chocolate chips over a double boiler on the stove or melt in the microwave.

3. Once melted, add a teaspoon of chocolate into each cup.

4. In a small bowl, stir the peanut butter, powdered sugar, vanilla extract, and salt. Place mixture into a plastic sandwich baggie.

5. Cut off a corner of the baggie. Squeeze the mixture into the center of each muffin cup.

6. Pour the remaining melted chocolate over the cups. Place in fridge until cooled.

– SASSY TIP –
Make a double boiler by placing a heatproof glass bowl over a pot of simmering water, making sure the water doesn't touch the bottom of the bowl. Stir in chocolate chips until ultra-smooth.

15

DESSERTS ARE A PIECE OF CAKE

What makes a party unforgettable? The cake! After slicing into these daring confections covered in chocolate frosting. your chocoholic friends will be asking for seconds!

DEVIL'S FOOD CAKE WITH CHOCOLATE FROSTING AND BROWNIE-STREUSEL CRUNCH

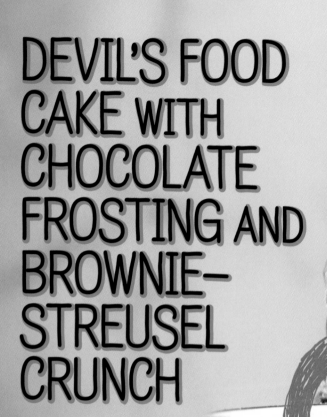

Sometimes chocolate cake with chocolate frosting is just not enough chocolate. Top off this dessert with a chocolaty crunch to fulfill all your chocolate desires...and then some!

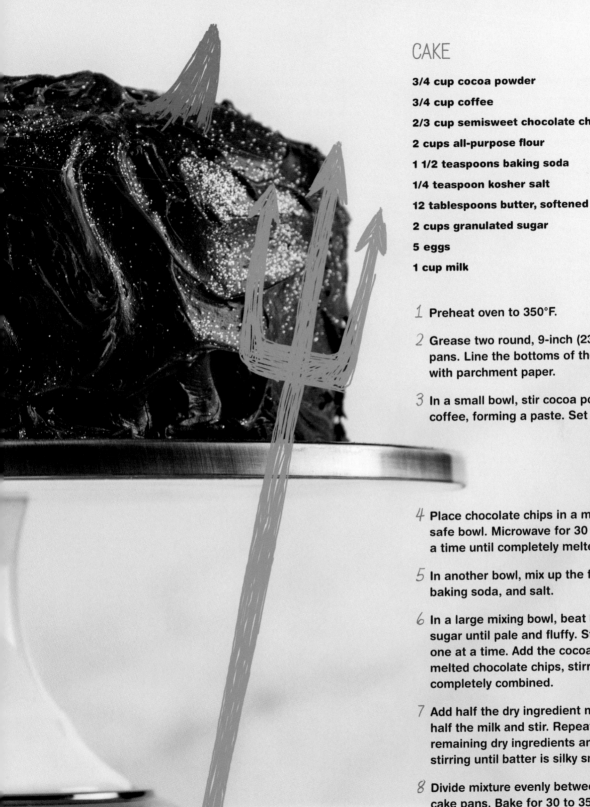

CAKE

3/4 cup cocoa powder

3/4 cup coffee

2/3 cup semisweet chocolate chips

2 cups all-purpose flour

1 1/2 teaspoons baking soda

1/4 teaspoon kosher salt

12 tablespoons butter, softened

2 cups granulated sugar

5 eggs

1 cup milk

1 Preheat oven to 350°F.

2 Grease two round, 9-inch (23-cm) cake pans. Line the bottoms of the pans with parchment paper.

3 In a small bowl, stir cocoa powder with coffee, forming a paste. Set aside.

4 Place chocolate chips in a microwave-safe bowl. Microwave for 30 seconds at a time until completely melted.

5 In another bowl, mix up the flour, baking soda, and salt.

6 In a large mixing bowl, beat butter and sugar until pale and fluffy. Stir in eggs, one at a time. Add the cocoa paste and melted chocolate chips, stirring until completely combined.

7 Add half the dry ingredient mix and half the milk and stir. Repeat with the remaining dry ingredients and milk, stirring until batter is silky smooth.

8 Divide mixture evenly between the two cake pans. Bake for 30 to 35 minutes, rotating pans halfway.

Recipe continues on next page.

FROSTING

1 cup heavy cream

2/3 cup granulated sugar

1 cup dark chocolate chips

1 cup semisweet chocolate chips

12 tablespoons butter, softened

1 In a medium saucepan, stir the cream and sugar together over medium heat, until sugar is totally dissolved.

2 Reduce heat to low. Add the chocolate chips. Stir until completely melted. Remove saucepan from heat.

3 Using a hand blender, blend butter into mixture, 4 tablespoons at a time, until smooth.

4 Let cool to room temperature before using.

CRUNCH

1 box brownie mix

1/2 cup vegetable oil

1 Set oven to 300°F.

2 On a Silpat®-lined sheet pan, use hands or a rubber spatula to combine brownie mix with oil until crumbly.

3 Bake 10 to 15 minutes until just set.

4 Let cool completely.

TO ASSEMBLE

1 Carefully remove devil's food cakes from cake pans. Place on a clean surface.

2 Using an icing spatula or butter knife, spread a thin layer of chocolate frosting onto the tops of both cakes.

3 Pile brownie-streusel crunch on top of one frosted cake. Then place other cake, frosting-side down, on top of streusel layer.

4 Spread a thin layer of frosting over the entire cake. Refrigerate until firm.

5 Once firm, spread final decorative layer of frosting over the entire cake, creating swirls or smoothing out as desired.

– SASSY TIP –
Add sprinkles for some more flaire!

OREO® CREPE CAKE

Crepes are a thin, pancake-like pastry that originated in France. They can be filled with anything savory or sweet. Once you make the crepes, the rest is easy. Just fill with whipped cream and crumbled Oreos.

CREPES

1/2 cup all-purpose flour

1 tablespoon unsweetened cocoa powder

2 tablespoons granulated sugar

1 egg

1 tablespoon unsalted butter, melted

1/2 cup milk

1. In a blender add flour, cocoa powder, sugar, egg, butter, and milk. Puree until well-combined and frothy.

2. Heat a 10- to 12-inch (25- to 30-cm) nonstick skillet over medium heat. Coat with butter. Pour 1/4 cup of the batter into the pan, swirl, coating the bottom of pan in a super-thin layer.

3. Cook until underside of crepe is golden, about 2 minutes. Loosen and flip to cook the other side for another minute or so. Set aside.

4. Repeat until batter is gone. You should have about 15 crepes.

Recipe continues on next page.

23

WHIPPED CREAM

1 1/3 cups whipping cream, cold

1/4 cup granulated sugar

1 teaspoon vanilla extract

1 Add whipping cream, sugar, and vanilla extract into a cold mixing bowl.

2 With an electric mixer, whisk ingredients on high until stiffened, about 1 minute.

OREO® CRUMBLES

7 Oreo® cookies, crushed

– SASSY TIP –
If you don't have Oreos®, try Thin Mints®, Fig Newtons®, or even chocolate chip cookies.

TO ASSEMBLE

1 Place a single crepe on a large plate or serving platter.

2 Using an icing spatula or butter knife, spread a thin layer of whipped cream onto the crepe. Then sprinkle a small amount of Oreo® crumbles on top.

3 Repeat layering crepes, whipped cream, and Oreo® crumbles.

4 Top it off with the remaining whipped cream and Oreo® crumbles.

RAISING THE BAR

Get ready to sink your teeth into exciting flavors, including chocolate (of course!), cinnamon, peanut butter, sugar, coffee, vanilla, s'mores, tea leaves, and candied ramen. These irresistible bars with unexpected ingredients are anything but boring.

S'MORE BROWNIES

No campfire required, but you can still sit in a circle and sing songs and tell ghost stories while these s'more brownies bake in the oven. They are just as fun to eat as original s'mores and even more delicious!

MARSHMALLOWS

3 packages unflavored gelatin

1 cup icy-cold water, divided

1 1/2 cups granulated sugar

1 cup light corn syrup

1/4 teaspoon kosher salt

1 teaspoon vanilla extract

1/4 cup powdered sugar

1/4 cup cornstarch

butter or nonstick cooking spray

– SASSY TIP –
Give your marshmallows wicked flavor.
Try adding dried lavender, cocoa powder,
or even powdered Tang®!

1   In a medium bowl, soak gelatin in a 1/2 cup of water.

2   Attach a candy thermometer to a small saucepan. Cook remaining 1/2 cup water, sugar, corn syrup, and salt over medium heat until mixture reaches 240°F. Remove from the heat.

3   Turn the stand mixer on low. Slowly combine the mixture from the saucepan into the gelatin mixture.

4   Change speed to high. Whip until mixture becomes thick, glossy-white, and lukewarm (about 12 to 15 minutes).

5   Add in vanilla extract and whip for an additional minute. Turn off stand mixer. Set aside.

6   In another bowl whisk together powdered sugar and cornstarch.

7   Grease a 13- by 9-inch (33- by 23-cm) baking pan with butter or cooking spray. Coat bottom and sides of pan with one-third of the powdered sugar mixture.

8   Using a rubber spatula, scrape marshmallow mixture into the coated pan. Spray spatula with nonstick cooking spray to avoid sticking.

9   Sprinkle one-third of powdered sugar mixture on top.

10   Let marshmallows set at room temperature, leaving them uncovered for at least 4 hours up to overnight.

11   Lightly dust a cutting board with the remaining powdered sugar mixture. Flip marshmallows out of pan onto the cutting board. Using a knife or cookie cutter, cut into desired shapes.

12   Dust with more powdered sugar, if desired.

STREUSEL

3 graham cracker squares, crumbled

1/4 cup brown sugar, packed

1/8 teaspoon ground cinnamon

2 tablespoons butter, melted

1 teaspoon vanilla extract

2 tablespoons granulated sugar

1/2 teaspoon salt

TO PREPARE

In a small bowl, use your fingers or a fork to combine ingredients until mixture resembles big crumbs.

BROWNIES

10 tablespoons butter

1 1/4 cups granulated sugar

1 cup unsweetened cocoa powder

1 packet, or 1 heaping teaspoon, instant coffee

1/4 teaspoon salt

1 teaspoon vanilla extract

2 large eggs

1/2 cup flour

1 **Preheat oven to 325°F.**

2 **Line bottom and sides of an 8- by 8-inch (20- by 20-cm) baking pan with parchment paper or foil. Make sure you have extra overhanging on all sides.**

3 **In a medium saucepan, mix the butter, sugar, cocoa powder, coffee, and salt. Cook on low heat, until the butter has melted and mixture is warm.**

4 **Remove from heat and stir in vanilla extract. Add the eggs, one at a time, whisking after each one. Add in the flour. Stir until completely blended.**

5 **Pour mixture into the prepped pan and spread evenly. Bake 20 to 25 minutes or until a toothpick inserted into the center comes out almost clean.**

6 **Let cool completely. Lift from pan using the excess parchment paper or foil. Place onto cookie sheet.**

TO ASSEMBLE

Top brownies with marshmallows and sprinkle with graham streusel. Have an adult torch or broil marshmallows until golden brown and streusel is lightly crunchy.

CHOCOLATE-PRETZEL TART WITH EARL GREY WHIPPED CREAM

What's better than mini tarts filled with delicious chocolate ganache topped with
fluffy whipped cream? Don't forget about the best part—the pretzel crust!
Each bite of this sweet and salty snack combines the best of both worlds.
Make the ganache and cream a day ahead of time and assemble the next day.

CRUST

3/4 cup butter

3 tablespoons granulated sugar

2 1/2 cups crushed pretzels

TO PREPARE

Mix all ingredients together. Press firmly into a greased tart pan.

GANACHE

3/4 cup heavy cream

1 packet (or 1 teaspoon) instant coffee

2 cups semisweet chocolate chips

3 tablespoons corn syrup

pinch of salt

1 teaspoon vanilla extract

1. **In a medium saucepan, warm heavy cream and coffee over low heat until steaming.**

2. **Remove cream from heat, add chocolate chips, and wait a couple minutes. Then stir until smooth.**

3. **Add the corn syrup, salt, and vanilla extract and stir again.**

4. **Pour mixture into the prepared pretzel-tart crust. Refrigerate for about 4 hours (preferably, overnight).**

5. **Serve cold.**

Recipe continues on next page. ⟶

WHIPPED CREAM

**1 tablespoon Earl Grey tea leaves
(from about 2 bags of tea)**

1 cup heavy cream

2 teaspoons sugar

1 **In a small bowl, stir Earl Grey tea leaves into
the heavy cream. Cover and refrigerate for
8 to 12 hours.**

2 **Strain the cream into a medium bowl. Press
on the tea leaves to extract as much liquid as
possible. Discard the tea leaves.**

3 **Whip the heavy cream with the sugar, or
refrigerate and whip up to a day later.**

SASSY FACT

Who was Earl Grey? He was, in fact, a real person. Earl Grey was the United Kingdom's prime minister from 1830 to 1834. Black tea flavored with bergamot was named after him.

CHOCOLATE FUDGE WITH WHITE CHOCOLATE CANDIED RAMEN

Fudge—it's guaranteed to be a sweet, succulent, sink-your-teeth-into dessert. Add candied ramen noodles on top for an unexpectedly perfect combination of gooey and crunchy. It's ra-mazing!

FUDGE

4 cups granulated sugar

1 cup milk

1 cup butter, room temperature

25 large marshmallows

2 cups milk chocolate chips

2 cups semisweet chocolate chips

2 ounces unsweetened chocolate, chopped

1 teaspoon vanilla extract

1 **Grease a foil-lined 13- by 9-inch (33- by 23-cm) baking pan with butter or cooking spray. Set aside.**

2 **In a large saucepan, stir together the sugar, milk, and butter. Boil over medium heat, stirring constantly. Once boiling, cook for a couple minutes without stirring. Then remove from heat.**

3 **Stir in marshmallows until melted. Stir in chocolate until melted. Add vanilla extract and stir until all ingredients are totally combined.**

4 **Immediately pour into prepared baking pan, spreading evenly.**

5 **Cool at room temperature for an hour or so.**

Recipe continues on next page. →

CANDIED RAMEN

**1 package instant ramen noodles
(discard seasoning packet)**

1 cup white chocolate chips

2 tablespoons butter

1 teaspoon salt

1. Preheat oven to 350°F.

2. Boil the ramen noodles according to the package directions. Rinse under cold water and drain to dry.

3. Spray a rimmed baking sheet with nonstick cooking spray. Spread ramen onto the sheet.

4. Bake for 30 to 40 minutes, turning sheet every 15 minutes for even baking, until ramen is golden-brown. Remove from oven and cool.

5. In a small saucepan, melt together white chocolate chips and butter over medium heat, stirring constantly.

6. Drizzle melted mixture over cooled ramen and sprinkle with salt.

7. Cool candied ramen at room temperature for about an hour.

8. Using a meat tenderizer or rolling pin, break candied ramen into small pieces.

TO ASSEMBLE

1. Top fudge with the candied ramen.

2. Cover and refrigerate for 3 hours or until firm.

3. Use foil to lift fudge out of pan. Cut into bite-sized pieces.

– SASSY TIP –
Uncooked instant ramen is a great after-school or after-work snack. Crush the noodles inside the pack, open, sprinkle on the seasoning, shake the bag, and enjoy!

JUST ADD SAUCE

What would cinnamon rolls or ice cream be without the sweet sauces that go on top of them? The perfect companion to a variety of desserts, these chocolate sauce recipes turn old favorites into showstoppers.

BUTTERSCOTCH PUDDING POTS WITH CHOCOLATE SAUCE

When you're in need of a rich and creamy dessert, look no further. Butterscotch pudding pots combine two sweet flavors into one saucy treat. Get ready for a butterscotch-chocolate blast!

BUTTERSCOTCH PUDDING

4 tablespoons butter

1 cup brown sugar, packed

4 cups heavy cream

1 teaspoon vanilla extract

1/2 teaspoon salt

8 large egg yolks

sour cream

Butterfinger®, crushed (optional)

1. In a medium saucepan, stir together butter and sugar over medium heat. Cook until the mixture starts to brown and smoke ever so slightly, about 15 to 20 minutes.

2. Slowly add the cream, a cup at a time. Cook butterscotch until any crystallized sugar dissolves. Add the rest of the cream, vanilla extract, and salt.

3. In a large bowl, whisk egg yolks continuously. Add some of the hot butterscotch cream while continuing to whisk. Once the yolks are warm to the touch, pour them into the pot of hot butterscotch and gently whisk.

4. Pour the mixture through a strainer to remove any solid pieces.

5. Preheat oven to 325°F. Place ramekins in a roasting pan or cake pan.

6. Divide the custard into the ramekins. Fill the pan almost to the top with very hot water. Loosely cover with foil.

7. Bake for 25 to 40 minutes or until the pudding pots are jiggly.

8. Remove the pan from oven. Let cool. Refrigerate for at least an hour.

CHOCOLATE SAUCE

1/3 cup dark chocolate chips

3 tablespoons heavy cream

pinch of salt

TO MAKE

In a small saucepan, stir all ingredients together over low heat until chocolate is melted and well-combined.

TO ASSEMBLE

Plop a spoonful of sour cream into each pudding pot, drizzle with chocolate sauce, and sprinkle with crushed Butterfinger®, if desired.

– SASSY TIP –
To separate egg yolks from the whites, crack open the egg. Let the whites fall into a bowl below. Move the yolk back and forth between the two halves of the cracked egg until all the white has fallen below. Save the whites for another use. Remember to always wash your hands with soap and water after touching raw eggs.

SASSY FACT
Adding water to the pan is called a "water bath." It helps the pudding in each ramekin cook evenly.

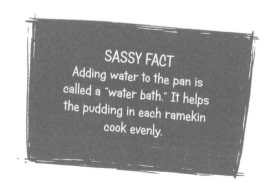

HOT CHOCOLATE FONDUE

How fond are you of chocolate? Whether it's a little or a lot, this easy-to-make chocolate fondue dipping sauce tastes great with bananas, strawberries, pretzels, or drizzled over ice cream or cake.

INGREDIENTS

1 cup semisweet chocolate chips

2 tablespoons butter

1 (14-ounce) can sweetened condensed milk

2 tablespoons coffee

pinch of salt

1 teaspoon vanilla extract

1 In a medium saucepan, melt down the chocolate, butter, milk, and coffee over medium heat. Cook and stir constantly until thickened, about 5 minutes. Remove from heat. Add salt and vanilla extract.

2 Serve warm as a fruit and cookie or cracker dipping sauce or drizzle over ice cream or cake.

METRIC CONVERSIONS

The measurements used in this book are imperial units. If you need metric units. check below.

TEMPERATURE

240°F	115°C
300°F	150°C
325°F	160°C
350°F	180°C

VOLUME

1/4 teaspoon	1.25 grams or milliliters
1/2 teaspoon	2.5 g or mL
1 teaspoon	5 g or mL
1 tablespoon	15 g or mL
1/4 cup	57 g (dry) or 60 mL (liquid)
1/3 cup	75 g (dry) or 80 mL (liquid)
1/2 cup	114 g (dry) or 125 mL (liquid)
2/3 cup	150 g (dry) or 160 mL (liquid)
3/4 cup	170 g (dry) or 175 mL (liquid)
1 cup	227 g (dry) or 240 mL (liquid)

READ MORE

Besel, Jen. *Baking Bliss! Baked Desserts to Make and Devour*. Custom Confections. North Mankato, Minnesota: Capstone Press, 2015.

Huff, Lisa. *Kid Chef Bakes: The Kids Cookbook for Aspiring Bakers*. Berkeley, Calif.: Rockridge Press, 2017.

Khan, Ramla. *Fairy Tale Baking: More than 50 Enchanting Cakes, Bakes and Decorations*. Northampton, Mass.: Crocodile Books, 2015.

Newquist, HP. *The Book of Chocolate: The Amazing Story of the World's Favorite Candy*. New York: Viking, 2016.

INTERNET SITES

Use FactHound to find Internet sites related to this book.

Visit *www.facthound.com*

Just type in 9781543530223 and go.

ABOUT THE AUTHOR

Heather Kim is a pastry chef, painter, and tattoo artist at Minneapolis Tattoo Shop, an all-female owned and operated parlor. Her deliciously unconventional desserts have been praised by the Minneapolis *Star Tribune*, *Minnesota Monthly*, and *Eater*. She lives in Minneapolis with her college sweetheart, Scottie, and their schnauzers, Max and Nietzsche.

Check out all the books in the Sassy Sweets series.

Compass Point Books are published by Capstone
1710 Roe Crest Drive, North Mankato, Minnesota 56003
www.mycapstone.com

Image Credits
Photographs by Capstone Studio: Karon Dubke, except: Shutterstock: 1989studio, 23 Right, Arayabandit, 6 Bottom Left, atdr, 4 Bottom Left, Becky Starsmore, 7 Bottom Middle, Diana Taliun, 15 Top, Iakov Filimonov, 6 Top Right, Jiri Hera, 29, Michal Schwarz, 4 Middle Left, Sean van Tonder, 6 Bottom Right, Shulevskyy Volodymyr, 40–41, VictorH11, 6 Top Left, W Photowork, 7 Bottom, wavebreakmedia, 4 Top Left, Yuliya Gontar, 2–3 Background, 4–5, 46–47

Editorial Credits
Abby Colich, editor; Juliette Peters and Charmaine Whitman, designers; Tracy Cummins, media researcher; Karon Dubke, photographer; Sarah Schuette, photo stylist; Laura Manthe, production specialist

Library of Congress Cataloging-in-Publication Data
Names: Kim, Heather, 1978– author.
Title: Beat it and bite it! : daring and divine chocolaty desserts / by Heather Kim.
Description: North Mankato, Minnesota : Compass Point Books a Capstone imprint, [2019] | Series: Sassy sweets | Audience: Age 9–11. | Audience: Grade 4 to 6.
Identifiers: LCCN 2018017828| ISBN 9781543530223 (library binding) | ISBN 9781543530278 (ebook pdf)
Subjects: LCSH: Cooking (Chocolate)—Juvenile literature subdivisions. | Chocolate desserts.
Classification: LCC TX767.C5 K55 2019 | DDC 641.6/374—dc23
LC record available at https://lccn.loc.gov/2018017828

Printed in the United States of America.
PA021